Color and Light

Text by Christine Pittel
Photographs by Dominique Vorillon
Design by Eric Baker Design Associates, Inc.

 Clarkson Potter/Publishers
New York

Donald Kaufman and Taffy Dahl

Color
and Light

Luminous Atmospheres for Painted Rooms

Photography and reproduction processes may cause colors to vary from the actual paint colors.

Copyright © 1999 by Donald Kaufman and Taffy Dahl
Photographs copyright © 1999 by Dominique Vorillon
Photographs on pages 8, 10, 13, 169, and 250 copyright © 1999 by Donald Kaufman
Twig house on page 11 designed by Jody Apple
Published by Clarkson N. Potter, Inc., 201 East 50th Street, New York, New York 10022.
Member of the Crown Publishing Group.
Random House, Inc. New York, Toronto, London, Sydney, Auckland
www.randomhouse.com
CLARKSON N. POTTER, POTTER, and colophon are trademarks of Clarkson N. Potter, Inc.
Printed in Japan
Library of Congress Cataloging-in-Publication Data
Kaufman, Donald.
   Color and light : luminous atmospheres for painted rooms / Donald Kaufman and Taffy Dahl. — 1st ed.
   1. Color in interior decoration. 2. Interior walls—Decoration. 3. Lighting, Architectural and decorative. 4. Exterior
lighting—Influence. I. Dahl, Taffy. II. Title.
NK2115.5.C6K37   1999
747'.94—dc21   98-44338
ISBN 0-517-70401-3
10 9 8 7 6 5 4 3 2 1
First Edition

Acknowledgments

One of the most difficult tasks concerning this book is adequately thanking everyone for their contributions and generosity. First and foremost we would like to thank all those who helped us take our pictures and allowed us to follow the light around their wonderful homes.

We wish to express our heartfelt appreciation to Joseph Giovannini, who provided our mass of disorganized information with the critical and insightful focus needed to make what we hope is a coherent whole.

Special thanks and gratitude go to Ann Forrest, who went far beyond the call of duty to assist us in locating our wonderful Southern California locations. Sidney Baumgarten, we thank you for your help and Lockwood de Forest lore.

Thank you, Phil and Helen Colcord, for guiding us to unique sites and arranging for all our practical needs.

Many thanks to Jack Holzhueter and his crew at the State Historical Society of Wisconsin, and to Joe Garton for his personal help and, especially, for his commitment and vision in saving the great resource of American theatrical and decorating history, Ten Chimneys.

Thanks also to Janet Jenkins at Robert Isabell for all her beautiful flowers, and to Eric Baker and Sabina Sieghart for their labors with the design.

This book would also not have been possible without the support and indulgence of many good friends, including Ellen and Peter Johnson, Phil and Judy Richardson, Chris Cozzarin, Joan Gers, Cynthia Conigliaro, and Suzanne Butterfield.

We would especially like to thank our editors, Carol Southern and Lauren Shakely, our art directors, Marysarah Quinn and Jane Treuhaft, and our all-important backups, Joan Denman and Camille Smith.

And finally, without the dedication and perseverance of our team, Christine Pittel and Dominique Vorillon, we simply wouldn't have a book. Thank you!

Contents

Veiled Light

Water Light

Stark Light

High Light

Amplifying Light

Animating Light

Coloring Light

The Path of Light

Color is light made visible.

Before the sun rises, the world is pale and wan. Only with daybreak will objects reveal their true colors. The paint in a room takes on a whole new character when sunlight darts across its surface.

Patterns of light we barely notice have a profound effect on how we perceive a room. Le Corbusier once defined architecture as the masterful play of light over forms in space. The quality of light in a space is so fundamental to our experience that it becomes the virtual fourth dimension of a room. Subconsciously, we recognize this primacy when we describe great buildings in terms of how they handle light. Designers will try to catch it, enhance it, reflect it, filter it, or otherwise exploit it.

Human beings feel a universal attraction to light. It is the source of life-giving energy, the property of the universe that God summoned first, the medium of prophetic revelation—and where there is light there is color.

Color is more than a film of paint on a wall. In scientific terms, a series of complex interactions between light, air, and surface culminate in our impression of red, yellow, or blue. The path of light starts at the sun. Perpetually in the process of nuclear fusion, the sun emits light that contains every wavelength, which means sunlight is pure white—the sum total of all the colors in the spectrum. But in the black vacuum of outer space, this radiance is energy alone and not yet luminosity. Light, in order to be seen, must strike something.

The sun's energy is first made visible when lightwaves hit the atmosphere that surrounds the earth like a forty-four-mile-thick skin of an onion. When the photons arrive at Earth's gaseous doorstep, they strike a range of tiny

molecules—predominantly oxygen and nitrogen—and light becomes color as the waves interact with the particles they illuminate. The sky appears blue because the shorter blue wavelengths have more chance of hitting something and being scattered—and therefore seen. Light has to traverse the least amount of atmosphere when its path is perpendicular to the earth's surface, which is why the sunlight at the equator is more intense and warm than the indirect sunlight at the poles, which must slant through more miles of air. Different hemispheric regions receive different degrees of light that produce different nuances of color. The light also changes according to the time of year. The light of winter in North America is cooler than the light of summer.

As the air thickens with molecules closer to the earth, light takes on local colors. In the tropics, water vapor combines with salt particles in the air to scatter and diffuse the light. On a hot, humid day at a Caribbean beach, the silvery mist of light will blur edges, while the sky on a day registering the same temperature in the high, dry desert of New Mexico will be a deep blue, the stark light outlining every object. In a dust storm in the red sand of the Arabian desert, light seems to phosphoresce. Man manufactures his own contribution to the atmosphere, and pollutants tint innocent light just as much as natural particles, usually shifting it toward the red end of the spectrum. In a city teeming with cars, a murky orange-brown haze settles in along the horizon. In Los Angeles, this lurid gloss can provoke preternatural effects—the sun setting over the Pacific ignites panoramas of surreal scarlet, saffron, and hot pink.

The air itself can seem colored. Distant mountains look blue because there is inevitably more blue light between you and a remote object. This blue veil is called airlight, which is simply sunlight scattered by the air molecules between you and the view. "Skylight" is the term physicists reserve for sunlight scattered by clouds and molecules in the sky. Most of the light illuminating our world is reflected. We rarely look directly at the sun. Instead, we experience its rays secondhand—bounced off buildings or the grass beneath our feet, scattered by all those invisible particles in the air.

When sunlight eventually hits the ground, it comes back altered. A Renaissance artist would add a hint of green to the face of a woman walking across a meadow. As in a theater, sunlit grass becomes a virtual uplight, tinting the air and everything it touches. Trees and plants in lush gardens have the same effect as they filter the sun through their leaves.

The light that lands on the windowsill, then, is layered—the result of many chromatic shadings on its journey from the stratosphere to the sidewalk. The influences only intensify as it enters a room. Curtains frame light and can shift its hue and temperature. A diaphanous fabric acts like a gel, coloring sunlight passing through.

Inside, light is a nimble captive of four walls plus the floor and ceiling, subject to all sorts of variations in surface from matte to mirror. "Material is spent light," said architect Louis Kahn, and every material reflects light differently. White paint scatters light uniformly in all directions, which is why it covers a

wall more efficiently than any other color. Glazed walls refract the light—bending each ray as it moves through two different mediums, from the translucent layers to the more opaque undercoat. (Whenever you glaze a wall, if you make the undercoat lighter and warmer than the topcoat, it will create a more luminous effect.) Dark woods absorb light. Metal, the most dense of all materials, is also the most reflective, especially when polished.

Colors, too, look different in different lights. A vivid rug that looked great in the clear, strong light of Santa Fe might seem garish in Manhattan, or a pale rug that showed all its colors in Charleston might go flat in Seattle. In bright light, we see warm colors more easily. Dim light brings out the cool colors, which is why blue flowers look more intensely blue at dusk.

A room becomes more pleasurable when you bring some of nature's effects indoors. Color in the sky is of a different type than color on the ground. It seems to float disembodied and dimensionless. Even when it becomes objectified by clouds or fog, it tends to softer boundaries and subtler shifts. These blurred transitions feel more atmospheric than sharper outlines. A gray sky is actually more luminous than a blue sky. Re-creating this luminosity in a room is as simple as keeping color values close. The less contrast of light and dark between hues, the more they tend to dissolve into one another.

Trees and rocks are composed of more opaque matter than clouds and fog, but their texture causes colors to break up in a similar way, giving us infinitely shifting nuances of warm and cool shades. We can juxtapose similar warm and

cool complements in our interiors for the same luminous effect. This is not a new trick. Landscape painters have employed this interplay for hundreds of years. Monet's flowers and trees achieve depth and radiance by being painted over a red ground. The key to any rich green is red. Complementary colors push each other away, heightening their contrast and emphasizing differences in hue that collectively create a full-spectrum range of white light.

The eye keeps trying to re-create white light. We fill in colors that are missing through afterimages. Our bodies want to bask in the white light of the sun, the energy source from which we evolved. The eye thrives on this atavistic reunion, and the most satisfying interiors merge warm and cool complements—applied to the walls or integral to the materials—to reconstitute the impression of white light.

The choice of particular hues is far less important than how they are combined into a delicate balance. Whether the palette is simple or complex, the interaction comes back to the basic polarities of light and shadow. We're so accustomed to seeing interiors in terms of objects that it requires a bit of readjustment to focus on the light. But light is the essence of color. Sometimes all you need to do is look out the window to figure out what colors flourish in your specific light. Take a cue from nature. Then, in every room, you will suddenly be able to see the light.

Veiled Light

Great architecture reveals light.
In different regions across the country,
styles have evolved to suit the local climate
and culture. Thick walls in a Southern
plantation house shield against the heat of
the day, and deeply recessed windows order
and control our perception of light.

Carolina Low Country

Sunlight strafes the mahogany double staircase and burnishes the wide pine floorboards at Drayton Hall, the first and finest example of Georgian architecture in America. Built on the banks of the Ashley River just west of Charleston, South Carolina, over a five-year period beginning in 1738, it was the country seat of John Drayton, a member of His Majesty's Council and heir to more than twenty rice, indigo, and cotton plantations. The stately two-story brick house stands on an elevated basement to evade the penetrating damp. A two-tiered Palladian portico —supported by Doric and Ionic columns carved out of Portland stone in England and then shipped—offers some welcome shade on a sultry day. ❡ After the Civil War, Drayton Hall was the only Ashley River plantation left standing since it had been a makeshift smallpox hospital (possibly a clever ruse) and no Union soldier was tempted to approach. But even more remarkably, it has

Back when Drayton Hall was built, the most efficient means of travel was by boat, and guests often saw the river facade first, OPPOSITE. You can peer right through the house from the front and back doors, which are perfectly aligned for cross ventilation. Now most visitors arrive by car, BELOW: Twin staircases on the facade lead down from the portico to the drive, which passes an ornamental pond.

PAGE 17: Walls painted with Prussian blue pigment dramatize the magnificent double staircase, hand-carved from West Indian mahogany, in the entrance hall.

survived the centuries practically untouched. From 1742 until 1974, when it was acquired by the National Trust for Historic Preservation, it had been in the hands of seven generations of the Drayton family, and no one ever tampered with it except to make basic repairs. (The original twelve-over-twelve pane windows blew out in an 1813 hurricane and were replaced with the then-fashionable six-over-six; the slate roof was redone with tin in the 1870s; bricks fell from the pediment during the 1886 earthquake and Victorian shingles were substituted.) Inside, there is no electricity or plumbing.

Open the paneled front door and step into the eighteenth century. In each high-ceilinged room you can almost hear the rustle of floor-length skirts or catch a whiff of tobacco as if spirits from another era have just vanished around the corner. The classical orders constructed inside—the tangible expression of Enlightenment reason, proportion, and man's will to measure—are still as harmonious as they once were. But time and southern humidity have left their fingerprints and revealed this strictly structured house to be an organism. The walls are gradually exfoliating as surfaces turn into a minute *craquelure* of paint. The architectural order verges on disorder, suspended midway between rationality and randomness, the man-made and the natural, now that every pilaster is sheathed in the ravaged beauty of peeling paint.

In more than 250 years, the interiors have been painted only twice—when the house was finished and again in 1870. In the magisterial Great Hall, with an overmantel copied from a design by Inigo Jones, the natural grain of the cypress paneling runs through the worn paint like a watery stream. The colors have also mutated with age. Georgian "white" was not the bleached

Ironwork was usually painted dark green to blend into the vegetation until black became popular in the late nineteenth century.

Madder brown paint articulates the hand-carved details.

These muted shades share the same tonality. Color values—just where on the scale of light to dark a color falls—are consistent. The eye is always making comparisons, moving from one point of contrast to another, and a room with subtle contrasts feels more atmospheric. Only the grandest eighteenth-century houses had moldings picked out in another color, as in the Great Hall, LEFT, with an overmantel modeled after one by English architect Inigo Jones. Sunflower and dogwood medallions alternate on the cornice frieze. RIGHT: The Palladian passion for symmetry produced this graceful enfilade of doors.

Drayton Hall was constructed long before central heating and every room has a fireplace. This eighteenth-century mantel has become a delicate *grisaille* of peeling paint. BOTTOM: Where the hand has constantly touched, surfaces are stripped of pigment.

white of today. Instead, it was usually mixed with a few shakes of earth pigments to give it a creamier tone. Furthermore, the linseed oil used as a binding agent for most oil paint tended to yellow over time. Colors mixed with the costly new Prussian blue pigment, invented in 1704 and derived from animal blood mixed with alum, can look almost green now. Warmed by the afternoon sun, the colors on the handsome paneled walls at Drayton Hall have mellowed into a consonant threnody of tones.

In these empty rooms, it's much easier to appreciate the light. With no distractions—in a drawing room stripped of furniture—you can trace the path of light across a hand-carved plaster ceiling and down a paneled wall. The architecture materializes the light, providing a backdrop for the mercurial play of sun and shadow—and the light reciprocates, revealing the volumes, planes, and details of the fine-boned architecture. Just as light, or the lack of it, can stimulate or stifle a color, the quality of the light has the power to transform the character of a room. Light is creating half the drama of this haunting space, and no discordant notes break the spell.

In a bare room, you notice the little events of light. Deeply recessed windows become glowing lightboxes, reflecting the sun from more than one side. The garlands over the drawing room windows were hand carved from the same mahogany as the staircase. On the ceiling, native plants were sculpted out of wet plaster, the first example of this technique in America.

Charleston

This red brick house in the historic district of Charleston, South Carolina, was built around 1738 by a fur trader who sold pelts from the porch. In the old days, before air-conditioning or central heating, a house by necessity related to the environment. This one is sited on a diagonal to the path of the sun so it can create its own shade. Deep porches, designed as open colonnades and known in Charleston as piazzas, extend the length of the house and block the direct light. Rows of windows and French doors open to the breeze. A fireplace in every room takes the chill off the winter mornings. ⸎ Occupied for generations by the same family, the house holds layers of possessions that could only have been accumulated over time. The mahogany sideboard, chinoiserie

PAGE 24: Except for brick pillars destroyed in the great hurricane of 1752 and replaced by painted wood columns, the George Eveleigh house has remained fundamentally unchanged since it was built about 1738.

OPPOSITE: Hanging a mirror across from a window to reflect sun and scenery is a familiar decorating technique, but here mirrors cleverly placed between the windows also reflect the reflection. ABOVE: A pattern of light overlays the floral pattern of the rug in the second-floor drawing room, where French doors open to the piazza. Beveled cypress paneling uniformly painted in pale green, RIGHT, becomes a neutral backdrop to both a china collection and the Adam-style mantel, salvaged from a neighboring house to replace the marble original, which was broken in the 1886 earthquake.

Olive velvet drapes temper the light in the dining room, ABOVE, where almond green walls set off the dark mahogany furniture. Gilt wood valances help to compensate for the seasonal lack of sun in the ground-floor study, RIGHT. Warm colors raise the temperature in winter.

chests, cloudy mirrors, and tattered silk curtains add more mellow tones and texture to the paneled walls, carved moldings, and mantels, whose slight irregularities bear witness to the hands that originally crafted them and the passage of centuries. The atmosphere of a house caught in aspic —the clock stopped here somewhere in the 1920s, or was it the 1820s?—is as palpable as the atmosphere outside, where the South's high sun smolders in air heavy with humidity and salt particles from the nearby ocean. Hazy light hovers at the windows like a veil.

The mood could easily be broken by harsh colors and high contrasts. Instead, the ambiguous hues inside reinforce a fugitive atmosphere built on the fragility of patina. In the living room, celadon green walls and shell pink curtains are as ethereal as the barely perceptible patterns on the faded silk upholstering the Louis XV chairs. Complementary colors like pink and green set up their own subtle dynamic. The pink softens and warms the bright light slanting through the windows. Green is a diplomatic color in the middle of the spectrum—cool enough to feel sheltering in this climate and warm enough to work with the dark, burnished woods. A ground-floor study that gets less light and can be cold in winter is painted a golden yellow.

The filtered light, caught for a moment in the glint of a well-bred crystal chandelier or the gleam of family silver, never overpowers the alluring blur of old gilt. This is a house that cherishes shadows.

Light is captured and held by silver and gold. These candlesticks, goblets, and gilded frame draw light deeply into the dining room. The sterling silver ancestral sword on the sideboard was made by Tiffany & Co.

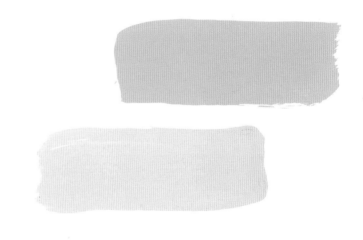

OVERLEAF: A crystal chandelier at once disembodies and materializes light, LEFT. Multiple reflections and refractions create its sparkle. Embroidered Chinese silk and old wallpaper blur into a lustrous image, with even more shimmer due to the patina of age, RIGHT.

The second-oldest city in South Carolina, after Charleston, Beaufort is a small, languid enclave on one of the southernmost Sea Islands. Since it fell into Union hands early in the Civil War, the town was spared by General Sherman during his flame-lit march to the sea. The long economic slide ever since also helped save many of its antebellum mansions from both the bulldozer and Formica kitchens. But some of the patrician houses protected by the benign neglect of urban decline suffered the indignity of being subdivided into apartments. That was the fate of this Georgian dowager, originally built in 1786, and the task facing its new owners and their architect, Jay Dalgliesh, was how to make it whole again. Color played a major role in bringing it back to life. ¶ A warm, rich palette was chosen to compensate for the cool character of the coastal light. The low-lying islands here are fringed by salt marshes. Diffused by the salt particles suspended in the air, sunlight

Beaufort

PAGE 33: The exterior of the house is a pictorial composition of two straightforward colors and one complex texture. The beige, pink, and violet tones of the tabby finish on the facade set off dark bottle-green shutters that integrate the house into the landscape, BELOW. To preserve the period look, only handmade glass panes were used in the restoration of the windows.

is bleached out and softened: on some days the air outside turns white and the horizon line blurs. Soft, mellow colors suit the soft air. Specific hues were determined by the orientation and function of each room. The library looks out on majestic live oaks dripping with silvery gray Spanish moss, so the walls were painted a pale gray-green to relate to the foliage. Deep apricot flatters the features of those seated around the mahogany tables in the dining room next door. Views from room to room should also be considered when choosing colors, and complementary hues like apricot and green used in conjunction enhance each other.

Although the long depression stripped the house of some original details, time did leave a patina. The owners appreciated and understood the weathered beauty of the exterior stucco—a local cementlike concoction called "tabby," made of oyster shells, sand, and lime—and left it as is. The walls in the upstairs ballroom hadn't been touched in decades. The worst bits of flaking paint were scraped off, then the remainder was touched up with a thinned-down, oil-based primer and brushed with two coats of a tinted translucent glaze. The acrylic glaze gives the variegated walls a slight uniformity of color in a silvery gray-green range, while allowing the *pentimento* of previous lives to seep through. The crazed pattern of the old paint underneath imparts a natural texture, reminiscent of snakeskin or tree bark. The combination of texture and translucency makes the surface particularly responsive to the shifting light.

White trim accentuates the handsome Georgian details. On the back porch, the white-painted columns and railings pick up a green tint from the trees.

Bits and pieces of pearlescent oyster shells account for the subtle glow of the original tabby. Its crumbling condition telegraphs the house's age at a glance.

OPPOSITE: The original wood paneling in the parlor, sold off at a low point in the house's long history, was tracked down in San Francisco and brought back for reinstallation.

When the house was built, cooking was done in a separate anteroom. A new kitchen, in the former dining room, retains an old-fashioned air. Buttercream walls make the original heart pine floors look even more mellow. Cupboards were crafted from more heart pine to look as if they had been there forever. The cabinet holding the soapstone sink was painted gray.

Pale gray-green walls in the library, ABOVE, defer to the more colorful dining room just beyond. A square bay, RIGHT, lets more light into the dining room and holds the smaller table. Warm apricot paint puts an attractive blush on the face of even the most pallid dinner companion. Moss green curtains, the perfect complement to the apricot, puddle on the floor.

The few pieces of furniture in the ballroom only accentuate its emptiness. Attention focuses on the perimeter and the fine architectural details, enhanced by a translucent glaze. The paneling below the windows slides open for ventilation, LEFT. Crazed paint provides an infinite number of reflective surfaces that create their own iridescence, not quite so bright as the mirror, ABOVE.

for such anachronisms as air-conditioning. The owners, avid sailors, preferred to throw open the windows to catch the breeze. Paint can also contribute to the fresh-air effect, since it is one way to control the visual temperature of a room. White feels cool in summer and accentuates the detail on the Federal-style wainscoting. Yet even within the simple palette of whites chosen for this house, shades fluctuate from warm custard to cool violet. The living room walls are a rich and inviting buttercream. The yellow tone helps balance the abundance of blue light reflected off the ocean (since water absorbs more of the sun's red rays) and brings the dominant impression of the room back to white.

Here on Cape Cod, white carries nautical associations that give a spin to how we see color. Think of spanking white canvas sails and salt-white deck cushions set off against dark varnished wood. In a coastal town steeped in seafaring imagery, ultramarine blue is a favored color for front doors as well as skiff bottoms. White trim works equally well for boats and houses. Frank Lloyd Wright once said that good architecture is like fine tailoring—it is the terminal points that matter. White eaves, window frames, and even wainscoting are the cuffs and collars that give a house definition. The structural connotations of white—with its suggestions of masts, beams, and bones—has shaped the New England vernacular. The color palette in this house respectfully draws on that tradition.

PAGE 45: Shadows of white timbers on the boathouse porch dial the time of day on the unpainted floorboards.

In the two-story-high entryway, OPPOSITE, bluestone from the path outside comes into the house and encircles an inlaid wood floor that suggests the points of a compass. White connotes structure and is therefore appropriate for the columns and the circular band at the second-floor level, which reiterates the circle on the floor. The dome above is painted violet white to conjure up a shimmering sky and bring the maximum amount of light into the hall.

In a house where rooms are designed to flow together, white serves as a transitional device, connecting the cool blue tones of the entryway to the warm pumpkin walls in the dining room, ABOVE. The unusual color was copied from the paint inside an antique cabinet, and links the piece to the room.

In the library, OPPOSITE, an ordinary window—as well as gilded wood—frames a maritime view. The chestnut paneling, salvaged from the original house, was rubbed with tung oil to bring out the latent color. Much of the woodwork in these coastal houses was crafted by shipwrights during the off-season.

LEFT: Silvery-gray shingles and white trim characterize the architecture of the New England coast. BELOW: In a living room with more windows than walls, all looking out on the ocean, there is a surplus of blue light. While water does not reflect light exactly as a mirror would, it does reflect about 50 percent more light than land. To counteract all this blue, the white walls are torqued toward yellow.

OVERLEAF: The sheen of the mahogany table echoes the effect of light on water, seen through the bay window's subliminal target. Salt particles in the air outside create a haze that blurs the distinction between clouds and sky.

Tethered to the shore by an arched wooden footbridge, a square white pontoon serves not only as a motorboat mooring but also as an outdoor living room for this compact boathouse commanding a bay in Maine, rebuilt on the original foundation and converted into living quarters by local designer Mark Umbach. The surrounding water influences the hue of the clear northern light, shifting it to the blue end of the spectrum. To compensate for the cool chromatic temperature, Umbach paneled the rooms indoors with traditional beaded board to turn up the thermostat on the light pouring through the many windows. ¶ Using wood is a clever way to have the effect of color without it being perceived as color. The warm tones of the knotty pine complement both the evergreens outside and the bay. Were the pine's orange hue simply

Maine Island

painted on the walls and ceiling, it would probably be too strong, but the pattern of the grain mitigates the intensity. The beaded slats produce thin shadow lines that give the surfaces a relief whose depth is accentuated by the sheen of the varnish. With nautical associations of an old-fashioned hull, the wood is also psychologically reassuring: the material projects the imagination onto the water, as though buoyed there by a classic sailboat crafted in the days before fiberglass.

Wood is shorthand for shelter and enclosure. By applying it to the ceiling as well as the walls, the designer creates a solid case for comfortable furnishings like the pillow-strewn couch and the wicker armchair in the living room. Green trim on the windows with shades to match brings the forest in. Lamplight fires up the walls and the red Oriental carpet. At night, the boathouse glows.

PAGE 53: Green trim on this former boathouse was a natural choice given the surrounding woods and Maine vernacular.
LEFT: Knotty pine walls and ceiling create a uniform perimeter, which visually stretches the boundaries of this small living room. The vertical thrust of the beaded boards is softened by the scattered knots, which add a secondary horizontal pattern.

Shingles are more akin to nature than almost any other building material. Grazed by light, which reveals every irregularity and imperfection, they resemble tree bark. The uneven wear on this facade, RIGHT, is a chronicle of local weather conditions. The upstairs bedroom is barely big enough for a bed.

With its graceful arches, the dock reads as a bridge connecting land and water, ABOVE AND LEFT. The square footage of the small house is augmented by the pontoon, which functions as a summer living room. The expanse of sky is doubled by its reflection in the still water, punctuated by the elongated dock.

With rolling fog banks and tumultuous cloud-bursts alternating with brilliant sun shining in clear blue skies, San Francisco routinely has more visible, changeable weather than perhaps any other major American city. The precipitous hills

San Francisco Bay

offer the perfect vantage point to view the daily spectacle of light, water, and dissembling fog. Since the city straddles a peninsula, no spot is very far from the sea. The cool blue light reflected off the bay shifts from green to violet, refracted through tiny water droplets in the air, which are constantly whipped by the wind to produce that extraordinary scintillating effect. The light in San Francisco seems alive. ❧ Choosing paint colors for the interiors of a venerable house atop Pacific Heights meant matching these outdoor atmospherics, in a sense, since a room is much more pleasant to be in if it relates to the exterior light. The dining room, with a six-paneled bay window facing the

PAGE 58: Poised between the weather of the ocean and the weather of the land, San Francisco has a dynamic climate. The abrupt difference between earth and water temperatures results in fog, which creates a constantly shifting backdrop as it rolls in over the bay. The sky becomes almost material and then, in an instant, the clouds dissolve. PAGES 60–61: Theatrical drapes in the dining room act as a proscenium, framing the view. Swags and jabots give the impression of curtains, without obscuring the bay.

Even on foggy days, a crystal chandelier, ABOVE, collects light. BELOW: The contrasting moldings ground the perimeter of the room.

water, was the logical place to start. Curiously, the most critical decision was not the actual color —often the particular hue comes last—but how saturated it should be. The intensity of the color had to correspond to the intensity of the light just outside the window. Fog can diffuse light so outlines blur, but paradoxically color can loom even more intense. The strong, flattering pink—not too white and not too red—has the same luminosity as the colors outside and, as a complement to those blue-green effects, it enhances the watery view. The upper register of the wall and the cove ceiling were painted a pale blue, so that the ceiling dissolves into the sky. Moldings painted buttercream are like the frosting on a cake, and the pale yellow brings the full spectrum of red, blue, and yellow primary colors into this one room. The eye moves easily across delicate contrasts that distinguish the architectural detail. The subtle transitions of hue are as fluid as the color and light variations among the fog banks outside.

If you mixed the blue-green color of San Francisco Bay and the yellow-green foliage, the result would be the green in the library, ABOVE. Painting the fireplace panel green as well was a bold stroke.

Lemon yellow paint intensifies the sunlight streaming into the living room from the adjoining sunporch, OPPOSITE. Red upholstery jumpstarts the color scheme.

In the sunporch, the pale cream paint on the sweeping windows dissolves the mullions into the view. The earth tones of rattan furniture and matchstick blinds act as a darker foil to the flood of light.

An apartment eight stories above the asphalt of New York may seem far removed from the finer points of nature, but not when the rippling surface of the East River casts quivering reflections on the high ceilings. Room after room feels suspended over the water, and the owners decided nothing should get in the way of this scintillating river light. The ephemeral effects could easily be eclipsed by elaborate curtains or competitive wall colors, so the rooms facing the river are decorated very simply to keep the focus on light and art. ¶ Both husband and wife are collectors of twentieth-century painting, sculpture, furniture, and glass. To show off their acquisitions and unify the main living areas, they chose a single color—pale caramel, which is a complement to the blue water—for the walls. Reiterated in slightly different intensities,

Manhattan

PAGE 67: The interior of a duplex apartment in New York is a study in chiaroscuro, with both direct and reflected light silhouetting the balusters of a curved staircase. OPPOSITE: The caramel palette expands to include mahogany, cordovan, and black in the dining room, where a Jean Dubuffet painting consolidates all the browns. Ceiling lights in the shape of glass flowers form a constellation over the diners' heads, and echo the sparkle of the river. RIGHT: Architects Rendell Fernandez and Simone Corno designed routed moldings to collect shadows and emphasize the sinuous curves in the foyer, where Venetian glass evokes the ever-present water.

the caramel—taken from a Fortuny fabric that panels the dining room—was as warm as the walls could go and still appear colorless. Accustomed to the Mediterranean light of his native Italy, the husband instinctively wanted to compensate for the coolness of the blue river light with a warm color, but in a neutral tone that would not clash with the art. The uniform perimeter creates a gallerylike environment.

The discipline of the understated color, reinforced by the spare refinement of the furnishings, combines into a serene composition that allows architectural features like the arched doorways and winding staircase to carry more of the weight of the decor. By minimizing distractions and maximizing the light, the owners effectively let the river run through the apartment. In this context, the glass collection seems serendipitous. It looks as aqueous as the water. Glass, like water, gets its color not only from light reflected off its surface, but from light transmitted and refracted from within. This increases the depth and richness of the color. When the sun strikes one of the pieces on display throughout the apartment, the glass seems to blaze from deep inside. By inference, the glass draws your attention back to the river outside, which turns the quiet drama of light passing through a window into a daily event.

The honey-stained hardwood floor belongs to the same family of hues as the caramel walls, reducing the visual contrast between floor and wall to keep attention focused on the artwork. A George Segal sculpture occupies the bay window.

OPPOSITE: A space-age version of the typical Venetian glass chandelier—designed by Giò Ponti—adds a jolt of color to the kitchen. The caramel, cordovan, black, and mahogany tones of the dining room are also integral to the materials here, but they look much more stark against white walls.

In an apartment where every piece of furniture is an art object—like this André Arbus stool beside the living room fireplace—the sophisticated palette is strong enough to make an impression of understated elegance, yet subtle enough to defer to such masterworks as the Matisse watercolor.

Sunlight brings out textures and colors that might otherwise be missed in the mono-chromatic master bedroom, where walls are painted deep caramel. In the late afternoon sun, a split-straw screen by Jean-Michel Frank looks almost iridescent. The mottled green surface of the shagreen desktop lamp glistens, and the Mario Bellini leather chair glows, as if lit from within.

It is a rare luxury to sit in the bath and watch freighters glide up the river. Shot through with light, an oversized perfume bottle turns into a semiprecious stone. The pale floating walls are brought down to earth by dark mahogany doors, which contribute a sense of gravity and age.

Whimsical blossoms by Ansola Fuga, OPPOSITE, bask in the river's bright light, which brings out every nuance of the handblown glass.

Mahogany paneling in the library, on the side of the apartment with no river view, substitutes the warmth of wood and the pattern of the grain for the dappled light off the moving water. Blood-orange blown glass by Dale Chihuly sets the fireplace aflame.

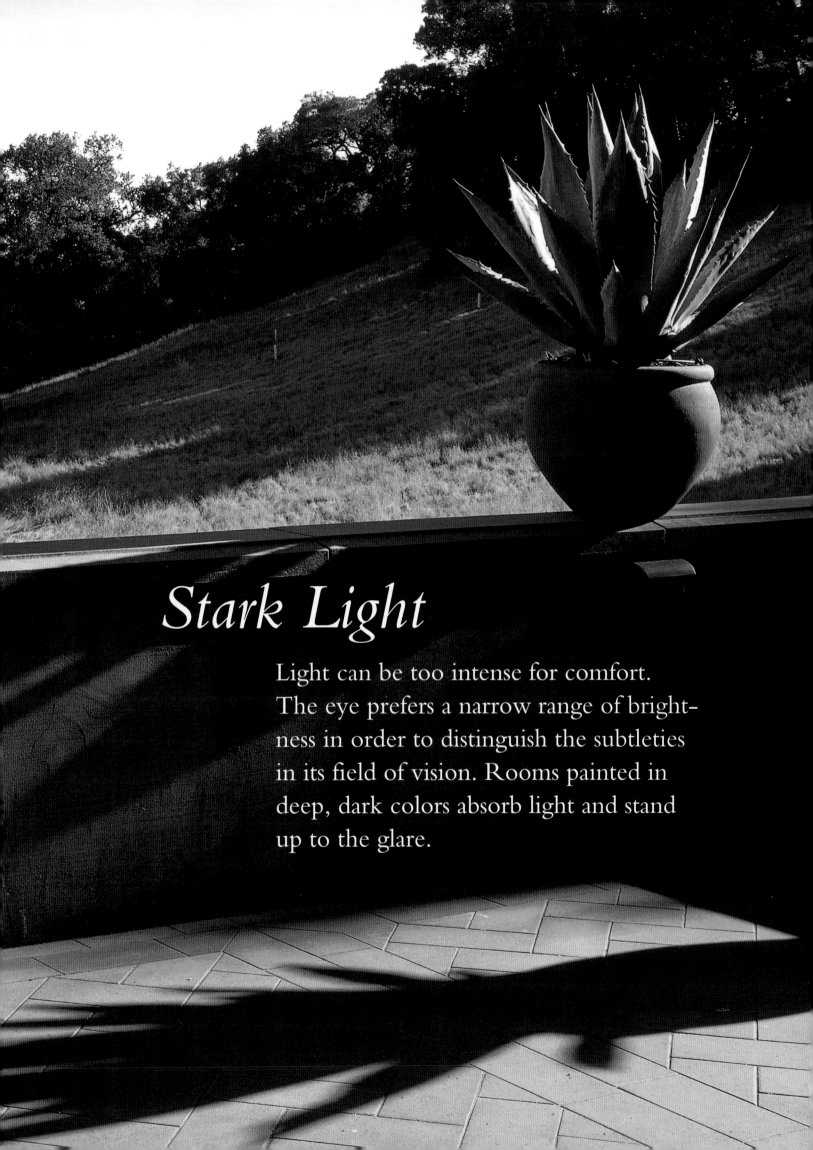

Stark Light

Light can be too intense for comfort. The eye prefers a narrow range of brightness in order to distinguish the subtleties in its field of vision. Rooms painted in deep, dark colors absorb light and stand up to the glare.

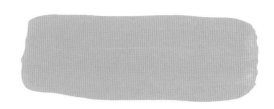

Sun Valley

The last thing this family wanted for their new house in Sun Valley, which is covered with snow most of the year, was more white inside. Ordinary white walls would only exacerbate the stark light. The cold blue light glinting off snow can have the brilliance of a floodlight. The blue cast occurs because water, whether frozen or not, absorbs more of the sun's red rays and reflects the blue. ❧ Color can counteract this relentless cool blue. Starting at the perimeter, red brick pavers on the porch combine with the dark wood rafters of the overhang to temper the light before it enters the house. The sandy brown stucco exterior walls, made from a local aggregate and integrally colored cement, sponge up some of the glare. ❧ Inside, the strategy was to warm the two main entry points of the

Snow, within its whiteness, is blue. We not only *see* blue as a cool color, we physically *feel* it as colder in temperature. When the light from the early morning sun is blocked by the mountains, the blue shadows that result are a combination of the blue-reflected sky light and snow's subterranean blueness. Later on, the sunlit snow is whiter.

PAGE 79: The matte surfaces of Idaho stone, unglazed brick, and textured stucco are the first line of defense, absorbing the bright light reflected off snow. The red window frame in the yellow mudroom, RIGHT, gives the blue light streaming in a warmer cast.

house, creating chromatic hearths where people can thaw their hands while taking off their coats. The marigold walls in the mudroom, which is the usual family entrance, seem to glow—offering a warm welcome as you come in from the cold. The Pompeiian red in the front foyer does the same, but with a more formal black-tie sophistication.

After these vivid colors, the hues progress to a more calming palette of earth tones. Colors as saturated as the marigold and red would be too intense for the main living spaces—especially when inhabitants are confined indoors for the winter. The baronial living room and family room—with high ceilings, natural beams, and imposing fireplaces—are painted, respectively, eucalyptus green and tan, colors just deep enough to help absorb the reflected glare and warm enough to counteract the blue cast from the snow while still remaining restfully neutral. A deep tea green creates a sense of intimacy in the library, while the children's rooms are painted traditional pink for the girl and beige for the boy. The variety in the colors of the interior environment revives spirits during the long hibernation.

Local architect Janet Jarvis took great care to make the new beams in the family room ceiling look old, ABOVE. Cordovan-colored concrete floors scored in a broad diamond pattern give a sense of weight and presence to the public rooms. OPPOSITE: Tyrolean motifs on the fireplace add delicacy to the timbered living room. RIGHT: The light reflected off the snow turns a tea green wall in the library almost blue.

Italian immigrants introduced grapes into the Napa Valley in the 1850s, so it should be no surprise that Italianate farmhouses eventually followed. Few, however, are as Palladian as this villa designed by Ned Forrest for vineyard owners who

Napa

first roamed the Veneto, measuring walls, studying proportions, and paying particular attention to color. The couple now bask in the glow of their research. In late afternoon, the California sun strikes their burnt sienna, umber, and ochre walls and the colors ignite, like a match flaring. ⸹ The solid, symmetrical house proudly presides over the landscape, yet never overwhelms the natural setting. During the hot, dry summers, its broad, two-story stucco mass dissolves into the

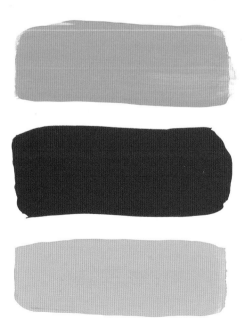

For the double-height living room, OPPOSITE, the late decorator Mark Hampton chose a rich, light ochre, deep enough to contain the volume and bright enough to register as luminous. The play of light from high square windows animates the upper expanses of the vast walls.

Early morning fog blurs colors and blends the house into the landscape as water droplets in the air scatter and diffuse the light. With hot, dry summers and cold, wet winters, Northern California's climate and vegetation resemble that of Italy. The Italian vernacular, as reinterpreted by architect Ned Forrest, looks right at home in the Napa Valley.

surrounding fields because it, too, is made from earth. Earthy colors like ochre absorb harsh light without bleaching out and defuse even a violent summer sun. The palette subdues California's penetrating Mediterranean light without making it cold. Strong colors make intense light tolerable and, conversely, intense light begs vibrant color.

The burnt sienna that marries the walls to the landscape contrasts with the lush, romantically overgrown garden immediately adjacent to the house. The garden may offer a cool refuge from the summer heat, but the main line of defense is the Mediterranean-style house itself, typically built with thick walls and small windows to shield the interiors from the sun. Wide eaves and generous porticos create a shady transitional zone between outdoors and indoors. Shadows play a significant part in climate control. But the drawback of this natural cooling strategy becomes clear on gray winter days, when dim rooms can feel lifeless and chilly. The solution? Compensate with color. A blood-red dining room seems to import its own personal sun. In spaces like this, saturated with pigment, even the shadows come in color.

PAGE 85: When sunlight hits the sienna walls under the fire engine–red portico ceiling, they turn orange and incandesce. Even shadows change hues in this color-saturated environment. Outdoor shadows are the result of the columns blocking the yellow light from the sun, leaving only the reflected sky light, which is blue. But reflected red light from the ceiling turns this shadow violet and makes the whole space vibrate.

The transition from outdoors to indoors is less abrupt when an interior as vibrant as the exterior reduces the contrast. In the dining room, ABOVE, light bounces from blood-red walls to the red-stained ceiling and terra-cotta floors, creating a warm bath of airborne color. Dark wood beams, OPPOSITE, put a lid on the jewel box.

A window treatment can transform a room by affecting the quality and quantity of the exterior light. Diaphanous fabrics make the passage of light almost tangible. Coral-and-white striped curtains frame French doors and subdue the bright morning light, casting a pink glow over the breakfast room.

ABOVE: Beyond the lily pond and just off the door to the kitchen, an outdoor dining room seems even more inviting because of subtle color interactions. The hues of terra-cotta walls and dense green foliage effectively push each other farther apart, making the sienna feel warmer and the green cooler. The complementary colors amplify each other.
RIGHT: The blue-violet acanthus is the exact complement of the terra-cotta wall.

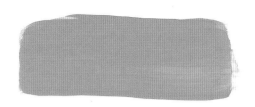

Serenity was the goal in the creamy white
master bedroom. On the adjoining terrace,
reflected light from the red eaves turns the
sienna walls orange, the terra-cotta tile pink,
and the gray door blue.

The color of a pool is influenced by the light reflected from its walls and bottom. Here, natural gray cement absorbs more of the red and yellow rays and causes the water to appear a deeper blue. The pool house, painted mud brown and overgrown with vines, blends into the setting.

The garden was created as a series of out-door rooms. In an intimate nook, LEFT, a tiny square opening in a vine-covered wall creates the illusion of a mirror or a picture, and reveals the sunstruck flowers in the garden room beyond. BELOW: A rustic pergola filters the light.

An alleé of trees along the path breaks and dapples light, ABOVE. The shadow patterns create the illusion of deeper perspective and greater distance. LEFT: The afternoon sunlight burnishes an antique chest and rustic pottery.

Architectural drawings line a hall, and the glass in their frames reflects and transmits the subdued light.

Nothing reflects more light than snow. Not even water—you could be on a boat, midocean, on a glorious summer day and it would not be half so bright as a sunlit field blanketed with snow. In the clean, clear mountain air of Ketchum, Idaho, anyone walking through waist-high drifts to get to this cabin tucked amid the trees might be dazzled by the brilliance. Snow scatters light in all directions, and there's something extraordinary about the resultant atmosphere—it sparkles. The tiny hexagonal ice crystals that constitute snow act as prisms, refracting the light rays. Imagine millions of microscopic mirrors, glittering like diamonds en masse and multiplying the normal level of daylight tenfold. ⸋ This complicates the transition between outdoors and indoors. After

Ketchum

PAGE 97: A lone bush gives an otherwise monochromatic, two-dimensional landscape depth of field. The exterior stucco, OPPOSITE, was mixed with local river-bottom sand to produce a dark, craggy surface that blends into the trees and subdues the brightness. The carmine red door complements the greenery.

Falling snow reduces the overall amount of light and scatters what's left so efficiently that all color turns to darkness or white.

such brilliance, it's difficult for the eye to adjust to the relative dimness of a room. Once you're settled inside, the view from the picture window will remain brighter. Since the contrast in levels of illumination is inevitable, local architect Dale Bates equipped the building with the equivalent of sunglasses to cut the glare. The exterior surface of the cabin is a dark, rough-textured stucco that absorbs light, bouncing less of it back through the windows into the rooms. (On the same principle, if you want more light indoors, paint your house and your neighbor's white.) The deep brown integrally colored stucco, matched to the bark of a fir tree, looks like another natural element within the landscape. Dormant shoots of red twig dogwood poking up through the snow are the same carmine red as the door. In the cold, dry air at this high an altitude, even the smallest hint of color registers. Bright, flashy colors would look artificial.

The projecting roofline acts as an awning and prevents some of the insistent light from penetrating inside, where there are only two rooms—a sitting area and a sauna. Both are clad in cedar, accentuating the connection to the trees outside. Most people don't think of wood as a color, but the honey stain on the cedar counteracts the cold blue light coming in from outside. The magic of wood is that it evokes warmth while absorbing light. Wood can be dark and still appear luminous. Like water on a rock, the glossy tung-oil finish brings out the rich colors in the grain. When sunlight strikes the wall, the wood comes to life and glows like banked embers. The designer has created a simultaneous condition of fire and ice.

A shadow is a volume of space shielded from the sun. The color of a shadow is a blend of reflected skylight and the surface it hits. The bluer sky, ABOVE, creates a bluer shadow. When clouds shroud the sun, RIGHT, shadows turn violet gray. Sun makes snow sparkle as the light is captured and dispersed through the prisms of the snow crystals. Like all white light passing through a prism, each sparkle emits every color of the rainbow.

Wood, too, has color. This cedar paneling ranges the spectrum from red to orange to yellow. Some people would find the equivalent color too garish were it translated into paint, but the variegation in the grain adds diverting texture. People will accept variegation in paneling, because they don't perceive it as a single color, but not in flat paint.

There is a reason, beyond the bougainvillea and the backyard pool, why people succumb to Los Angeles. One of the most arresting attributes of the city is the light—that strange, bright, dematerializing light that makes even a building seem oddly insubstantial. It's as though the photons were working their way into the skin of each

Los Angeles

object. Things lose mass as they're suffused with an otherworldly neon glow. ¶ Walking through this all-pervading, uniformly lustrous ether of light can be addictive. Ironically, pollution is one of the factors inducing this state of monotonous bliss. The light in Los Angeles is uniquely diffuse because there are so many particles in the air, scattering the rays. A day can be bright enough to

PAGE 103: Architect Paul Laszlo designed a broad veranda back in 1939 to shade the rooms and create plenty of outdoor living space. The horizontal shadow line from the extended roof accentuates the feeling of shelter. Light reflected from the lawn tints the columns and eaves green.

require sunglasses and yet there will be no shadows. Mountains can vanish when there are billions of particles between you and the view, each one bouncing the light like a mirror straight back at you.

Actually, the eye doesn't like so much uniformity (which is why fluorescent lights are unpleasant). It has nowhere to go for a rest. High contrast automatically draws its attention, but to keep readjusting from light to dark can also be exhausting. So the color scheme inside this 1939 Los Angeles house, one of the first to be built in exclusive Bel-Air, compensates for the diffuse light by creating its own contrasts within the narrow range with which the eye is most comfortable.

Modesty is not normally one of Hollywood's hallmarks, but this prewar house was built when every square foot counted, and the director who bought it and supervised the renovation respected its discreet character and scale. The long, low planes punctuated with wide windows and French doors were conceived to maximize exposure to the yard and let the outside in. Broad eaves protect the interior from the glare.

The front door opens to a foyer with two side vestibules. Straight ahead is the staircase next to glass doors leading to the rear garden. This multifaceted entryway was treated as a single volume and painted white, except for the gently vaulted ceilings of the vestibules, which were emphasized with a pale spring green. The green could almost be a reflection from the grass outside. The colored ceilings differentiate these transitional spaces from the rest of the house, in lieu of color on the walls, which would have interrupted the architectural flow.

Pale spring-green paint draws attention to the subtly vaulted ceilings of the twin vestibules on either side of the entrance foyer. Green, with its suggestion of foliage, was a logical choice for this transition space between outdoors and indoors. You can stand at the front door and look straight through the long, narrow house to glass doors, just beyond the stair rail, opening to the backyard.

In the living room, warm creamy beige walls reinforce the sepia glow from the wooden blinds. The mellow wood of the undulating Eames screen and straight-edged sofa compounds the effect. Dark upholstery adds built-in shadows.

Vibrant plum walls with gray trim keep the
dining room, OPPOSITE, from dissolving into the
garden by providing a strong frame for the
lush vegetation. Like a still pond, the glossy
black marble tabletop reflects the greenery.

To the left is the living room, where venetian
blinds made of honey-colored wood temper the
bright light and create a sepia-toned atmosphere
reminiscent of a film noir. Further on is the dining room, where lavender walls complement the
lush green foliage seen through the French doors.
Warm and cool polarities—like the honey-stained
floor and the lavender—energize a room. If you
want to re-create the effect of white light, you
need to add the color that's missing. Here, the
orangy (red and yellow) floor and green garden
needed the violet (blue and red) walls to add up
to the impression of white and fill out the
spectrum.

If you turn right from the front door, you
reach the library. The deep moss green on the
walls was taken from the color of an old cloth-
bound book. The dark wall sandwiched between
a light floor and ceiling expands the perimeter of
the room and offers a distinct change of pace. The
green also complements the violet at the other
end of the house, and both colors—more intense
than the rest of the rooms—terminate the color
sequence and put a stopping point on each end
of the main axis. Color reinforces the architecture
and relates to nature, with just enough contrast to
challenge the light.

The library was irregularly shaped, with a
green marble fireplace spanning a chamfered
corner. Moss green walls unify the space and
create a sense of enclosure. Painting the
cornice green, as well, raises a low ceiling.

Gutters painted to mimic verdigris match the green of the lawn and accentuate the dominant horizontality of the house.

A mirrored wall in the bathroom makes the space feel bigger—not only because the reflection visually doubles the square footage but also because images in a mirror appear to be half the size of the actual objects, making the reflected space look even larger.

Warm orange wood and cool gray-blue granite constitute complementary polarities in the kitchen. Renovation architect John Powell collected all the plumbing in visible freestanding pipes, so the rest of the island could gracefully float.

High Light

Up in the thin, cold air, colors take on an exuberant life of their own. Red looks redder and blue looks bluer when there are no pollutants between you and the hues. Even subtly different shades are easily distinguishable, and strong contrasts of color acquire a graphic clarity.

Lone Pine

These rocks may seem familiar. More than a hundred Westerns were shot here on a high plateau in the shadow of two mountain ranges, the Sierra Nevadas and the Inyos. A sentinel outcropping of boulders looks close enough to touch, but distances are deceptive in the cool, dry air. The absence of pollution at this elevation, combined with low humidity and strong winds, means that the outlines of objects seem crisper, with sharper contrasts between sun and shade. In this pellucid light, colors are clear and true. Designer Madeline Stuart could paint the interior of this gambrel-roofed house, surrounded by sagebrush and scrub, with ten subtle shades of brown and green and notice each variation. ℘ These earth tones were chosen to root the house in the landscape and create an atmosphere

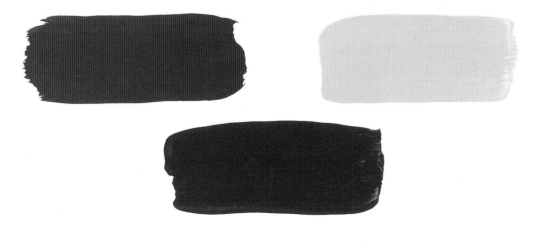

PAGE 112: With the sun at our backs, its slanting light is traveling through more atmosphere than when it originates from overhead at midday. This means more of its blue rays are scattered, leaving a higher percentage of red and yellow, which turns the tops of the Sierras bright orange.

for an undistinguished developer-built eyesore that had none of its own. River rocks were carted into the living room to add character to the fireplace wall and weathered barn wood was fashioned into an Arts and Crafts–style mantel. Sage green walls set off with olive green trim make the space feel cool even on a day when it's 102 degrees in the shade. Chamois-colored wainscoting confers instant age.

Stairs painted rust red—a color lifted from local wildflowers and the complement to the green—lead up to a wainscoted hall painted the same calm green and cream as the ground floor. Turn left to a master bedroom painted the yellow of dry grass or right to a guest bedroom, glowing violet like the sky at dusk. Yellow and green complement violet, but there is another layer of logic to this scheme. When the sun rises, the cool purple in the eastern bedroom cuts the penetrating glare. On the other side of the house, the master bedroom is still in shadow in the morning and the warm yellow paint compensates for the dimness.

Taken straight from the surroundings, the understated palette in the house spans the spectrum from red to violet in subdued gradations, just as the color of the rocks outside subtly shifts from sunlit red to smoky violet over the course of a day.

OPPOSITE: A small staircase acquires depth and substance after the treads are painted rust red, a color inspired by the milk vetch growing wild outside, ABOVE. The reflection from the red turns the cream wainscot pink.

Rustic textures and naturally occurring colors like sage green and sandy brown bring the landscape, ABOVE, into the living room, RIGHT. The ridges of the sisal carpeting catch the light and evoke an image of real ground. When color is integral to the material, as in the river-polished rocks surrounding the fireplace or the stained pecan mantel, it registers less as color. But that warm pecan note dominates the room and makes it feel as mellow as worn saddle leather.

Yellows and greens evoke sunshine and foliage in the kitchen, where the shade is drawn for a moment against the dazzling morning sun, OPPOSITE. The range of tones—from the chartreuse cabinet to the banana yellow stepladder chair to the manila shade to the cream wainscot—mimics the gradation of foliage. ABOVE: Walls are painted the color of the hard-packed earth outside the back door.

The view from the bedrooms suggested what color each should be. The master bedroom picks up the greenish yellow of the grasses on the western side of the house. In the hallway, neutral green mediates between the warm yellow master bedroom and the cool lavender guest room.

The rock formations beyond the porch off the east-facing bedroom, LEFT, turn violet between 5 P.M. and 7 P.M.—just when a guest is likely to withdraw to this room, OPPOSITE, to rest and change before dinner. The pale lavender on the walls blurs right into the twilit sky.

OPPOSITE: Sage and shrubs rooted amid the
rocks show the effect of arid conditions.
Moisture travels to the top leaves, which
turn green, leaving the lower sections gray
and violet. Close examination of the color
reveals just as much yellow and violet as
green, but we are culturally conditioned
to perceive almost all plants as green.

Adjacent colors in the spectrum blend into each
other, which is why this green hallway flows so
easily into the yellow master bedroom.

The high contrast of the dark wood cabinet against the grooved wainscot in the upstairs bathroom draws the eye, while the flat cream-colored wall recedes into the background. The dark object also pushes the light colors closer together in value.

"It's a different kind of color from any I've ever seen," said Georgia O'Keeffe, who painted the stark landscape and claimed it as her own. There is something uncanny about the light in Santa Fe. Piercingly bright, it seems to sculpt the old adobe houses into abstract

Santa Fe

planes against the cobalt blue sky. Science can explain why the sky looks bluer here than anywhere else, but the physics give no hint of the magic. At an elevation of seven thousand feet, the air is thin and dry and blissfully free of pollution. The thinner the air, the bluer the sky, because there are fewer air molecules to scatter all the different colors inherent in sunlight. The shorter, bluer wavelengths are much more likely to strike a molecule and be scattered—and made visible— than the longer reds. Consequently, more red

Handhewn ceiling beams called *vigas* create
their own shadow play in the library, filled
with Pueblo pottery and Navajo rugs.

PAGE 125: A gently rounded adobe wall
shows the touch of the hands that shaped it
out of the earth. The high barrier closes off
the open end of the U-shaped compound
and creates a secluded courtyard. Heavy
wooden doors at the entrance gate open to
a gravel drive.

wavelengths eventually hit the earth—rich in red iron oxide—and the intense light bounces back, creating a warm pink glow low to the ground.

Then the radiant pinks and bracing blues interact to produce iridescent greens and violets. Each permutation in hue is immediately perceptible due to the lack of particulate matter in the air. Colors are preternaturally vivid. The Franciscan friars, who arrived in the 1600s to build missions among the pueblos, named the mountains to the east Sangre de Cristo—blood of Christ—because at sunset their slopes flush flaming red in the Technicolor sky.

Shadows are razor sharp due to the lack of diffusion by the thin atmosphere. The normally fuzzy line of demarcation between shadow and sunlight is narrowed and made crisp. The thick walls and rounded edges of the local adobe vernacular are actually the perfect foil for this fierce light. Traditionally, earth was scooped up on the site, mixed with water and straw, and then baked in the sun to make adobe bricks. These were patted into place to form cavelike walls often two or three feet thick, which kept the house cool in summer and warm in winter. Small, high windows discouraged intruders and the light.

The original core of this adobe house dates from the early 1800s, but it has been expanded over the century into a U-shaped two-story compound with Spanish-style balconies and porches overlooking a wide courtyard. Still, it typifies the way adobes handle incoming light with kid gloves. Inside, sunlight is softened and diffused as it bends around curved corners. The gentle contours feather the light into even gradations across the customary whitewashed walls. The warm honey tones of pine ceilings and floors warm up rooms filled with simple, handcrafted wood furnishings. Living in an adobe offers the comforting sensation of burrowing into the landscape. Indoors, the transfiguring light of Santa Fe is soothed by the earth.

A painting by Arthur Dove hangs over the traditional rounded fireplace, called a *kiva*, tucked into the corner. Rather than staining the new pine floors, the owners rubbed them with linseed oil and let them age naturally.

OPPOSITE: The wide porch, festooned with chiles, offers shelter from the relentless Santa Fe sun that, as Georgia O'Keeffe said, "burns through to your bones."

The dining room, ABOVE, is one of the original four rooms of the house. Thick adobe walls act as natural baffles for the light streaming through the small window. Without whitewash, the room would be very dark inside. LEFT: The basic structure of the house is revealed as ceiling beams poke through the exterior walls and cast sharp shadows in the pellucid light.

OVERLEAF: The landscape is the source of materials for adobe construction and also the inspiration for the earthy palette.

The stainless steel in the kitchen looks almost warm since there is so little natural wood there to make it seem cold by comparison. The owners restored the restaurant stove that came with the house.

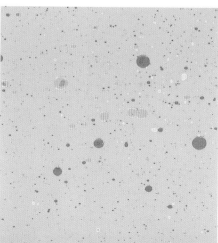

The terrazzo tabletop, OPPOSITE, inspired the whimsical floor, spattered with drops of orange, peach, and pink paint, LEFT.

Bounced within a banyan tree, sunlight
intensifies. In nature, what first appears gray
is really blue or green or violet.

Nature is the best colorist. Orchids
spontaneously growing on trees add red
and yellow to the blues and greens
and fill out the spectrum.

The skies of Puget Sound are perennially over-
cast, but instead of compensating for the elusive
light with such bright colors as yellow or red,
designer Jean Jongeward turned the weather to

Puget Sound

her advantage. Like
the Dutch painters,
she understood the
possibilities inherent
in a single ray of light, recognizing that the gleam
of silver is especially beautiful among the shadows
of a dimly lit room. ❧ In this classically detailed
1924 house, Jongeward matched the cloudy fore-
cast by choosing cloudy, ambiguous colors that
seem to melt into one another. Colors close in hue
and value—meaning they fall in roughly the same
place on the scale of light and dark—can create a
sort of atmospheric mist. Surfaces shimmer. At
first glance, the palette in the living room may

PAGE 147: Subtle permutations of color cultivate, rather than compete, with the light. Sun striking an apparently simple palette of taupe and cream creates rich gradations of darkness and light. Dark gray paint against putty-colored shingles, LEFT, brings out the architectural details of this Craftsman house with a classical bent.

seem monochromatic. But the longer you sit, the more you see the differences in color and appreciate the subtle transitions from taupe to sand to dove. No violent leaps across the color chart overwhelm the play of light. Every shift in the sun registers on these light-sensitive walls—like a shoji screen darkened by a passing cloud.

Reflective surfaces are unobtrusively integrated into the composition to lure the light. Any stray beam is captured and revealed in the sheen of ancient Chinese porcelain, the glint of pewter, the glistening glass-topped tables. Floor-to-ceiling mirrors planted in the corners dissolve the boundaries of the room as they ricochet every faint ray of light. Occasionally a high-gloss ceiling magnifies the shine and adds the illusion of height.

In the dining room, a moody seascape hand-painted on silver paper is as delicately drawn and tinted as a Chinese scroll. Sometimes the surface of the painted sea, just like Puget Sound on a hazy day, evanesces into pure light. Actually, a cloudy sky is more luminous than a clear sky—but that is a truth Jongeward already knows.

In the living room, taupe walls, dove trim, and a sand ceiling set up variations within the monochromatic theme. Glossy white window frames pivot the available light from outside to inside. Mirrors turn a corner and become surrogate windows, reflecting the outdoors.

Both ceiling and floor in the dining room extend the atmosphere of the mural by continuing the colors. The mottled checkerboard pattern painted on the floor creates its own motion, just like the cloudy seascape. A mirrored detail on a door matches the corner cabinet and captures the light from the windows.

The silvery sheen of the mural is more pronounced in the dim early morning light, which makes the whole room feel as though it is veiled in fog.

Light seems to linger in the glazed Chinese porcelains. Just beyond the spiral staircase, the library with its bay of windows gets the most light, so this room is painted the deepest shade in the series of beiges.

The slate-colored tiles around the fireplace, all close in hue and intensity but never quite the same, cue the palette. The yellow sun shining through Seattle's typically gray blue clouds gives a gray green cast to the light at various times of day.

The gray light of Seattle can be stingy, giving
little back in the way of color and luminosity.
So designer Terry Hunziker decided to transform
the dull light in his own loft
by designing in all the missing elements. He integrated
color into the jutting planes

Seattle

that turn the space into a three-dimensional de Stijl
painting and used common materials in unconventional ways to focus attention on their texture
and sheen, which accentuates the available light.
❡ A runway of hot-rolled steel slices the maple
floor into unequal halves and separates the living
and dining areas. The unexpectedly soft, velvety
quality of the steel contrasts with the highly polished plaster surface, tinted oxblood red, of a freestanding wall just above. This slab of wall inserts

PAGE 155: Planes of solid color separate and define the space without interrupting the flow. Light reflected off the steel strip between the living and dining area tints a biscuit-colored wall blue. The watery reflections of the Sally Mann photographs in the polished red plaster add a sense of depth to the hard slab.

the warmest color into the center of the room and works as a luminous core. Perimeter walls are either recessed or projected forward so that they, too, read as independent planes and catch the light. One plane of maple migrates from the floor to an inset in the ceiling, activating the space with integrally colored materials in all three dimensions. The floor, ceiling, and walls are designed as equal parts with equal weight in the visual composition.

As the planes construct the space, they color the light. It's possible to get away with more contrasts of color than you could in a conventional painted room because so many of these slabs read as elements of architecture, and we're not accustomed to thinking of steel or maple purely as color. In an approach that supplements the natural light coming through the windows, the designer has broken the space into planes of vibrant color, and the eye reconstitutes the hues into a luminous whole.

The ceiling inset is the same maple as the floor, but it looks yellower because it is illuminated by incandescent lamps, while the floor—illuminated by daylight—looks bluer.

Intriguing textures in the bedroom compensate for Seattle's soft light. On a mottled plaster wall between painted columns, a concrete shelf cantilevers out from steel wainscoting that continues down across the floor, bordering sisal carpeting. The metal's dark surface becomes a deep pool of reflected space.

The bathroom, OPPOSITE, presents a variety
of textures within the same color and value
range. BELOW: Raw wood, soft leather, brass
nailheads, and speckled shagreen reveal all
the richness of their subtle colors in the light.

Dishwater light can provoke drastic measures. Floral designer Robert Isabell literally razed the roof on his New York City home to create the consummate exposure and dramatize the nonde-

Greenwich Village

script urban light. In a three-story Greenwich Village building that once held six apartments, he gutted the interiors and then put a glass greenhouse roof over the shell. Open to the sky, the top two floors are now one huge master bedroom that acts as a sundial. All the ephemera of the day —the stir of leaves on the trees, the shadow play of the roof grid—register on the naturally white plaster walls in a visual haiku. The seamless high-gloss epoxy floor looks like liquid sky. ℘ No room with an ordinary roof could showcase light with

this much impact. Because the sun streams in from above, rather than laterally through the windows, its effects are particularly intense and pervasive. The glass roof broadcasts the rays evenly throughout the space, which becomes a vessel of light. Streamlined furnishings in gray or white, raw wood, or sandblasted metal establish a cool, monochromatic palette that keeps the focus on the light.

A slender second-story glass bridge hovers over a glass-roofed courtyard—planted with bamboo shooting up forty feet—and connects to another house in back. Again, Isabell defies expectations by opening spaces ingeniously to the light. A cement-walled, glass-roofed room filled with palms turns out to be a shower with a view of the sky. A translucent corrugated plastic wall gives another bathroom an eerie, underwater glow. White plaster walls, subtly tinted with violet or moss green pigments, seem to radiate more color in certain lights.

Clarity reverts to murk in the subterranean grotto, dug out from the basement, where the flicker of candles against rough stone walls is magnified by a bevy of mercury glass bowls. A back room reveals Isabell's secret for anyone who hasn't already figured it out—he is really a collector of light. Each drawer in a tool chest is filled with hundreds of different lightbulbs. The light sources in this composite dwelling are just as unconventional as the architecture and range from lanterns to Lava lamps. The man who turned his house inside out, like a sock, so that every interior space became an exterior space is really decorating with light—both natural and artificial. Even after the sun sets, the rooms glow. Lamps with globes in every conceivable shape and hue gather like luminous bouquets of flowers in various corners. Light metamorphoses into color.

PAGE 162: On either side of the interior courtyard between the two houses, lamps in all guises create penumbras of color. Rough concrete walls and luxuriant plants make a room with a shower, ABOVE RIGHT, feel as if it's out in the open air. BELOW RIGHT: A collection of cocktail shakers proves metal has many colors. OPPOSITE: Ivy unexpectedly cascades down the master bedroom wall.

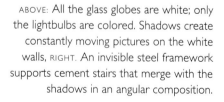

ABOVE: All the glass globes are white; only the lightbulbs are colored. Shadows create constantly moving pictures on the white walls, RIGHT. An invisible steel framework supports cement stairs that merge with the shadows in an angular composition.

OPPOSITE: In most rooms, people don't notice the ceiling. Here, the rush of clouds or the quiver of leaves beyond the glass catches every visitor's attention. A topless room creates a soaring sense of space. Furniture seems to float on the epoxy floor, whose shade varies with the color of the sky. Sandblasted glass windows face the street. Conceptions of interior and exterior space are constantly inverted.

The remnants of a blacksmith's forge and a bolt tether for horses were found in the basement, which was excavated down to the stone and deliberately left dim. A collection of mercury glass creates the illusion of more light.

Some passersby peer in, think this is a temple, and leave offerings at the front gate, RIGHT. The hanging lamps in the entry corridor were made from gourds, BELOW.

OVERLEAF LEFT: A Lucite chair looks like a ghostly emanation against a moss green plaster wall. OVERLEAF RIGHT: The zigzag stairs levitate over a steel console by Paul Evans.

Animating Light

Light is affected not only by the color of
a wall but also by its texture. Different
surfaces break up and reflect the rays in
different ways. Sunlight may stream or
spread or skip across a wall, depending on
the texture, and inert materials suddenly
take on the nuances of nature.

Some people might assume it takes a multitude of colors to create a rich and vibrant atmosphere; designers Stephen Sills and James Huniford required only one. White is the color of most walls in their weekend retreat just north of Manhattan, but because of the intriguing assortment of surfaces, the white paint interacts with light to convey a breadth of shades. The whiteout begins on the exterior walls of the 1929 American colonial manor and brightens the light bounced into the house. Natural elements like the lush green lawns and lofty trees absorb more sunlight than man-made materials like brick and cement, so the white paint maximizes the light that's left. Indoors, white appears in so many permutations that it simply becomes the lightest of many shades of pale. Chalk white hand-grooved plaster walls create vertical shadow lines that visually lift the ceiling in the living room and curve up at the

Westchester

PAGE 174: White shutters on a white facade signal something different about this house. Instead of presenting the usual contrast of colors, designers Stephen Sills and James Huniford explore the infinite possibilities of white-on-white.

In the living room, a Cy Twombley painting hangs on hand-grooved plaster walls that lift the eye and create their own shadow play.

The nuances of green in a mass of leaves, ABOVE, can be just as alluring as a multi-colored bouquet. As the light changes over the course of a day, upholstery segues from graphite to pale gray, giving substance to shadows. Pickled chestnut walls in the entrance hall beyond the living room, RIGHT, represent the warmer side of white.

In the library, on an eighteenth-century mahogany desk from Germany, a glass ball and stone amphora display opposite reactions to the light—the shiny surface reflects it and the matte absorbs it.

top in a distinctive cove. Sand-colored French limestone paves the ground floor and reinforces the note of antiquity. The rough, pitted surface of the stone is made up of millions of tiny facets that break up the light, creating the myriad color variations that give the floor depth.

The house is a tour de force of texture, a design stragety that appeals to the eye because it duplicates nature's effects. In each room, provocative textures—pickled chestnut, sisal, integrally colored plaster, bamboo slats, antique glass—fragment the available light and shift the colors subtly. The modulations approximate the shimmer of light on natural elements outdoors. You could count a hundred different shades of green in an iridescent meadow of sunlit grass rippling in the breeze. Textured surfaces create permutations of color and mimic the sensation of light.

But it takes a virtuoso to create so much variation within such a narrow band of color. It's as if Sills and Huniford deliberately limited their palette to show off their skill. Against the cool backdrop, furniture reads like sculpture. Each exceptional piece is more exquisitely proportioned than the next. In the drawing room, two Louis XVI ammunition cabinets flank a low-slung silk-covered sofa, across from an Empire recamier by Alphonse Jacob. The Neoclassical furniture is arranged like a three-dimensional still life within a spare, Modernist concept of space—which sets up an interesting dynamic. Each piece is perfectly poised, surrounded by plenty of breathing room. The chiaroscuro of dark wood against light floors and walls creates its own animation.

Then, just when you think you have Sills and Huniford pegged, they throw out all the stops and lacquer the master bedroom and bathroom walls a startling pond-scum green. This is defiant decorating that works by manipulating and exalting the light.

Bamboo blinds washed with white paint, ABOVE, mask the contents of shelves. OPPOSITE: The color of the silk taffeta curtains —fluctuating from gray to blue to violet—is as ambiguous as the sky.

Fearlessly, the designers rest a refined Louis XVI gilt bed on rough bricks in the guest-house. A hand-stenciled mosaic of shimmering paint creates as much textural interest on the ceiling as the bricks do on the floor.

ABOVE: On a black marble mantel in another guest room, the arrangement of objects in kindred colors is a tone poem. A Ming vase rubs shoulders with a rusty African snake. A table covered in Moroccan fabric, LEFT, sets off eighteenth-century Swedish chairs upholstered in worn silk velvet that catch the light.

Leafy trees enclose the house in summer, and several coats of paint have immersed the master bedroom, ABOVE, in green year-round. Curtains and sisal are dyed to match the walls. An Italian Empire steel bed, draped with a purple tartan blanket, gleams in the shadows. Squares of light from the windows reflected in the high-gloss paint blur into reflections from a family of eighteenth-century Dutch mirrors. OPPOSITE: The same green, braced with white, continues into the bathroom where a beveled wooden wainscot dignifies the space.

The whites in a simple collection of creamware, OPPOSITE, show an endless variety against an equally pale wall. A sleek banquette covered in creamy patent leather re-creates the same sheen in a totally different material. LEFT: The cloudy mirrored door and the waxy finish on the integrally colored plaster walls add the patina of age to the dining room.

The gravel courtyard establishes a white base for the white house and sets it apart from the landscape.

Santa Barbara

Santa Barbara is privileged for more than social reasons. Situated on a westward jog in the California coast, its pastoral hillsides face south and bask in the sunny exposure. The light, conditioned more by the ocean than the land, is pure and clear, with little particulate matter in the air since the city is surrounded by lettuce and artichoke fields rather than heavy industry. In fact, the balmy microclimate is almost identical to that of the French Riviera and can support an astonishingly wide range of plants. ❡ Back in the 1920s, during Santa Barbara's heyday, every newly minted millionaire's estate came complete with an equally elaborate garden, and some of the most distinctive were designed by Lockwood de Forest. Yet his own comparatively modest house and garden, begun in 1926 on a mere acre, achieves some sublime effects. A landscape architect trained at Harvard, de Forest had no compunctions about

PAGE 187: The square house, formerly owned by Lockwood de Forest, is built around an interior courtyard ringed by a wide hallway where one whole side is glass. This hallway becomes a virtual sundial, with light raking across certain sections at certain times of day.

Aluminum radiator paint dating from the 1920s has oxidized into a pale pewter shade on the dining room walls and ceiling, BELOW. At night, when the candles in the chandelier are lit, the reflections quiver. The single paneled wall, OPPOSITE, was washed with a silver gray stain to sustain the sheen.

On the wall where Carol Geyer's painting hangs, ABOVE, alternating swathes of hand-troweled ochre and gray plaster create depth and materialize the light.

mixing native plants and exotic species as he stretched the boundaries of European formalism to suit the rugged California terrain. He took similar liberties with his house, which grafts a Spanish colonial onto a Roman atrium plan and then modernizes the hybrid with lots of glass to cultivate the sun. Practically square in shape, the house is built around a central courtyard open to the sky, which doubles the perimeter of the house and the quantity of light. A broad hallway rings the courtyard and opens to the rooms, effectively giving each a double exposure since the courtyard side of the corridor is a wall of glass.

On the corridor's interior walls, de Forest hand-troweled the surface with integrally colored plaster in alternating coats of pale ochre and pearl gray. The coverage is purposely uneven, with variations of color and texture. The result is a moiré effect that shimmers—creating nebulae of light that animate the walls. In the course of a day, as the sunlight streams over the variegated surfaces, the balance shifts between warm ochre and cool gray. But the change does not really resonate as a difference in color. Instead, it draws our attention to light itself.

We follow the path of the sun, and the quality of light becomes the subject of the house. The rooms feel calm, shadowy, sheltered—making the transition to the bright garden outside all the more dramatic. Each room is plastered or painted in next-to-neutral shades, enacting the same subtle play between the polarities of ochre and gray, gold and silver. The color becomes warmer in the yellow kitchen, and cooler in the silvery dining room where the walls and ceiling are painted with aluminum radiator paint. After more than fifty years, it has the mellow patina of fine antique sterling.

Within this reduced palette, color does not distract from the ephemeral ballet of light across the walls. Struck by the sun, the two basic shades break up and recompose in constantly changing combinations. The gradations give the interiors a serene, dream-state softness, creating rooms distinguished by tones alone.

The courtyard at the center of the house features a ledge faced with polychromatic tile from India. More pale ochre plaster walls provide a demure backdrop for the exuberant furnishings in this bedroom, OPPOSITE, which opens to a lush green lawn.

The dining room represents the silvery pole of the palette, but in the kitchen the scheme swings back to gold. Plaster walls painted golden yellow, OPPOSITE, acquire more depth when juxtaposed with cabinets painted gray. ABOVE: The original countertops have mellowed with age.

Owners Carol and David Geyer are
gently restoring the house, but not tamper-
ing with its character. The original striated
plaster walls initiate the chromatic dance
of pale ochre and pearl gray that
makes up the subtle palette.

Two paths in a landscape—one in the garden designed by Lockwood de Forest surrounding this house, BELOW, and the other painted by his father, LEFT, reveal the poetry of dappled light. In de Forest's gardens, formal structure never quashes the exuberance of plants.

The magnificent feature in this Manhattan apartment just above the treetops, facing north onto Central Park, is the two-story-tall, room-wide window. But it was also part of the problem. Even towering, to-die-for spaces can

Central Park

suffer the flaw of frontal light coming from a monopoint, which typically happens in straight-and-narrow New York apartments or town houses sandwiched between party walls that offer only a single bank of windows on the street. In this situation, it's necessary to give dimension to the flat and shadowless light. North light, which is uniformly diffuse and indirect, compounds the blandness. This steady, consistent light traditionally preferred by painters does not automatically make a space feel good to be in. The original dark

oak paneling in the apartment, which was built as an artist's studio, aggravated the problem. Not only did it sponge up the available light, it also halved the space visually. The high waistline kept the room from adding up to a single volume. Inevitably, the eye goes to the point of greatest contrast. Reducing the contrast of the wood to the wall would allow the eye to focus on the more subtle contrasts within the paneling grid. But the consistent grain of the oak denied the sculptural relief of the paneling. The raised grid was an essential element in the plan to trick the shallow light into creating animated patterns and give depth to the walls.

The solution was paint. Many people think painting wood is a sacrilege, and everyone involved thought long and hard before taking a brush to the oak. Beige, even a range of beiges, hardly amounts to a rainbow. But beige in several gradations was all it took to modulate the incoming light and create the visual relief that even a subtle pattern provides. There was no need for a panoply of color. Beiges a cappella on the ceiling and the walls unified the space while counteracting the monotony of the light.

Now the putty-colored paneling shifts to a slightly darker bisque on the cornice-height molding and then a paler champagne on the plaster above. The ceiling is yet another shade of beige —lighter, with a yellow undertone. The darker cornice line bands the room and the slight chromatic variations introduce variety across the planes. By eliminating the homogenizing oak grain, the beige makes the shadow lines of the raised rails and stiles in the paneling more visible. Together, the barely differentiated beiges articulate a hierarchy of parts in the room from floor to ceiling.

Previously, the paneling darkened the room but now the beiges send light deeply into the apartment, like sound bouncing off the carved walls of a concert hall. The sculptural relief also fragments the light, so that it ricochets into the room at different angles. Beige, a mixture of red and green, is both warm and cool simultaneously. Now the space offers the best of both temperatures, as well as stimulating light.

PAGE 197: A monochromatic palette emphasizes the serenity of a symmetrical seating arrangement centered on a patriarchal fireplace.

The original dark oak paneling, OPPOSITE, was painted beige, with a slightly darker shade on the cornice-height molding, to unify the two-story-high space and bring out the sculptural relief of the grid. ABOVE: The view from the wall of windows in the living room takes in all of Central Park.

The ceiling of the dining area tucked under the loft was painted a lighter shade than the living room ceiling to draw more light into the compressed space. Flat paint was used for the plaster walls and ceiling, while the paneling is set off with a satin finish.

A Coromandel screen introduces subtle pattern to counteract the uniformity of the north light. Set at a right angle to the window wall, the screen breaks up sunlight hitting its folds into a montage of shadow and shimmer.

In the upstairs loft, the railing matches the color of the perimeter walls and expands the apparent size of the space.

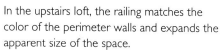

The paneling's rails and stiles, ABOVE, are the equivalent of acoustic baffles, breaking up light. An ornately carved chest accomplishes the same goal on a smaller scale. RIGHT: The cast stone mantel adds more texture in the same tones.

Coloring Light

Light not only colors a room, a room
can also color the light. Red paint on a wall
actually tints the atmosphere red. A full
spectrum of complementary colors re-creates
the white light found in nature.

Color begets color. One strong color demands the visual company of another—a fact few know better than Alexander Julian, a fabric and furniture designer famed for his exuberant palette. But

Connecticut Woods

how many people would be brave enough to follow his example and paint their own home with fifty-six vibrant hues? ℘ The cedar-shingled, hipped-roof five-bedroom house with dormers and bay windows and innumerable French doors was designed by San Francisco architect John Marsh Davis in the Arts and Crafts tradition that also inspired Frank Lloyd Wright. But this gracious reprise of a much-loved aesthetic is wittily subverted by a plunge into the hot bath of color. Julian's wife, Meagan, decided she wanted a kitchen the color of saffron when it's first stirred into risotto, and the scheme took off from there. A pink dining room leads to a crimson, milk

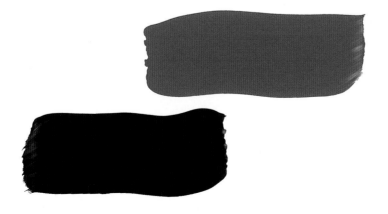

chocolate, and indigo blue living room. Crimson was chosen for the twenty-two-foot-high cathedral ceiling because it was strong enough to stand up to the multiple mahogany crown moldings and put a cap on the unusual room, taller than it is wide.

The stair hall just off the front door is a Fauvist fantasy, with each wall painted a different color—cornflower blue, chartreuse, coral. Teal was chosen for the upstairs hall because it worked well with the green reflections through the windows from the foliage outside and was bright enough to substitute for it in the winter months. A pink wall would have been grayed out by the green cast. Complementary colors subdue one another when mixed and, conversely, intensify one another when juxtaposed. You have to think of the color on a wall as being mixed with the color of the light hitting it.

The large planes of individual color in the stair hall also interact with one another. The coral wall throws coral light on the chartreuse wall, which then bounces over to the blue. In a sense, color hovers off the walls and mixes with other colors. There is an invisible sphere of radiant energy in the middle of every room that is a certain color and creates the atmosphere. By choosing a full spectrum of colors for the individual planes within a room, Julian is actually reconstituting the ideal—white light.

If you want to use a lot of different colors in one room, make sure they are all of equal intensity. Each of these distinct planes is equally saturated, and they don't seem disorienting

PAGE 207: Only a muscular framework could keep all these colors in check. Eggplant-colored paint on the eaves and trim is the violet complement to the orange mahogany. Grass tints the eggplant green. The stairway, LEFT, pinwheels with planes of color that never turn a corner. Because this is a transition space, the walls could take colors you wouldn't necessarily want to live with—like "scream-machine green," as Alexander Julian dubbed the chartreuse. Baseboards, trim, and risers are gray and the handrail is chocolate brown.

because probably 50 percent of the color we see is wood—but we don't think of it that way. Floors, doors, window frames, cabinetry, and furnishings occupy that range of wood tones we don't recognize as color. Culturally, we interpret wood as a material. Optically, we read it as a color along with the paint. The strong color planes do not throw the space out of balance because, according to the equal intensity principle, the mahogany trim that threads through the house is just as intense as the paint.

The bedrooms upstairs play the same game, in a lower key, with more subdued versions of lavender, yellow, green, and blue. Color used as planes in transition spaces becomes a container in these rooms. Once again, there's the mix of widely varying complements, with the difference that all four walls in one child's room are painted lavender and in the other, green, with the complements reserved for the trim. Then, since the rooms connect through a bathroom, they also complement each other.

The mood is more restful in the master bedroom, where Julian chose the soft colors you would find in sand or a shell, made even more opalescent by a layer of wax on top of the paint. The walls are a range of pale shades, echoing the generalized temperature of the natural light as you move around the compass—the wall that gets the western light is painted the warmest color. But the differences are so subtle that the room still reads as a whole. Through an adjoining door is the only white room in the house—a walk-in his-and-hers closet.

The natural light is more noticeable in the master bedroom, where colors are calmer, but of course the sun has been a participant in this drama all along. Ironically, the light that pours through the generous French doors and windows and brings these kaleidoscopic planes of color to life is also completely upstaged by them. Hues this aggressive seem to overwhelm any outside influence and create their own singular light. In this house, color is so intense it becomes almost palpable. The pulse quickens.

Multiple crown moldings in the living room, OPPOSITE, layer the soaring space. The crimson cathedral ceiling is balanced by another primary color—indigo blue—which backs the bookshelves and defines the panels above and behind the Tom Holland painting. On either side as you enter this "cathedral" are two "chapels"—anterooms painted chocolate brown. This shade, ABOVE, with a lot of red in it, is a reminder of the often overlooked range of browns.

The saffron paint in the kitchen, an unusual twist on yellow, manages to seem both earthy and bright at the same time. Cherry cabinets and countertops look even warmer in the reflected glow.

When a blue pine cupboard is set against saffron walls, ABOVE, the complementary shades intensify each other. The kitchen, which opens into a family room, BELOW, is the heart of the house and is painted in the warmest color. The raised fireplace in the family room is used for grilling in the cooler months.

Old-fashioned claw-foot tubs help suggest this is an old house in which bathrooms have been retrofitted. Violet on the window walls in the master bedroom, LEFT, cools the warm morning light.

Moldings picked out in periwinkle blue, LEFT, frame this pistachio green bedroom. The children's rooms, BELOW, painted in complementary shades, work as a suite of colors with a yellow connecting bathroom.

Architect John Marsh Davis blended a big
house into the landscape, ABOVE, with
mahogany window frames, cedar shingles,
and a shake roof. The elongated dining
room, OPPOSITE, with a wall of French doors
on either side, is the spine of the house. The
pink paint is as vibrant as the autumn leaves,
LEFT, and the high-gloss finish reflects the
shimmering flames of the gaslit sconces in a
room with no electrical lighting.

Penobscot Bay

Since this Colonial Revival house was built on an island in Maine in the 1920s, several generations of the same family have had the advantage of time to live with and perfect the interiors of this summer retreat, though "perfect" may not be quite the right word. Perhaps "personalize" better describes their casual approach to decorating. Every piece in the house seems to have been chosen by someone who loved it, whether or not it happened to fit seamlessly into a room. The result is an exuberant jumble of pattern and color, balanced by the rich, dark tones of burnished wood. ❡ Actually, a lot of color is not necessary to enliven light and make a space feel attractive. No matter how neutral the paint color or treatment, light is always affected by walls. The plaster walls and ceiling, left natural gray in the living room, add interesting texture. Along with

The plaster walls and ceiling, left natural gray, add a rustic element alongside the finely carved paneling in the living room. Multi-colored curtains warm the light as it enters, and a flower-strewn hooked rug adds another pattern to the sisal-carpeted floor.

PAGE 219: The delft blue on the facade of this Colonial Revival house could have been lifted straight from the sky. White-painted bricks have weathered into a soft rose.

the finely detailed mahogany-stained paneling, they create an earthy atmosphere and subdue the bright light in a room with windows on three sides. The wood also suggests shelter and protection and makes for an introverted room. But in this case, bold reds, blues, and yellows in the furnishings draw the room out of the shadows and recolor the light.

Anyone who could paint the exterior of their house a delft blue that rivals the sky obviously couldn't be content to stop there. So all the floors in the house are also painted—in colors ranging from chocolate brown to vermilion, with the more vibrant hues reserved for the smaller, transitional spaces, like the bathrooms and staircase. The high contrast between vermilion stair treads and yellow risers, or blue clapboard and black shutters merely echoes the high contrasts visible everywhere outside, in nature. Walk out the front door and you see green grass against blue ocean, and orange seaweed tossed against purple mussel shells. In the clear, bright air of Maine, where shadows are sharp and every hue registers, colors have punch.

Recently, the current owner discovered beautiful hand-painted Chinese wallpaper under a layer of plaster in the dining room and painstakingly disinterred it. The rich, multicolored wallpaper with vistas of maidens, mandarins, and pagodas against a lemon yellow backdrop transformed the room. The eye simultaneously sees fragments of shape, texture, and color and mixes it all up into a visual mélange that, like a Pointillist painting, adds up to a luminous whole.

In the foyer opposite the front door, floorboards were laid on a diagonal and the painted checkerboard takes advantage of the angled lines. The original beams were left exposed to contain the ceiling's extra height.

Handpainted Chinese wallpaper, ABOVE, opens the dining room to another view. RIGHT: The tiny white flecks—imprints of age and the departed plaster—increase the atmospheric effects.

The original dark chocolate brown paint on the living and dining room floors, OPPOSITE, takes away the materiality of the surface. The rooms become almost bottomless—as if the occupants were walking on water.

Self-effacing shades of beige—tan, sand, and ochre—on the walls and floor set the stage for the flower-bedecked Venetian furniture in this bedroom.

Like a pointillist painting, the bathroom wallpaper reflects more light than if all the separate colors were mixed into one shade. The Prussian blue–painted floor cools the room in summer.

There's a lot of color, ABOVE, lurking under the water when the tide recedes. Crab claws and seaweed lend their hues to the stair treads, RIGHT.

On the bay, colors differ under-foot depending on the time of day. When the tide is out, there will be thirty more feet of rocks and sand, heaped with greenish-brown seaweed.

Colors have to be strong to stand up to the harsh Florida sun—and not just figuratively. This is where paint companies come to test their latest

Palm Beach

products against the elements. As you get closer to the equator, the angle of the sunlight becomes much more direct, relentlessly beating down on bathers and buildings from straight overhead for much longer portions of the day. If a color survives here, it can survive anywhere. Neither the bold violet nor the saturated mango on the facade of this Palm Beach residence seems to be in any danger of fading meekly away. Under these hot, humid conditions, intrepid color becomes a matter of integrity. The owners heightened the hues of this house to compete with the lush vegetation and the cerulean blue sky, so that all are equal parts of a chromatic composition in which nothing drops out. The color bar is set consistently high across the tableau. ❡ Decorating is basically

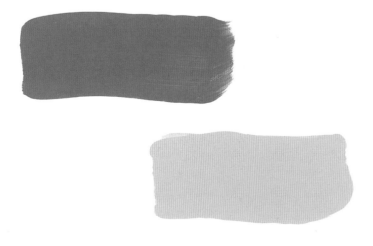

a balancing act. Turning up the color volume outside has consequences for the interior. Colors have to be similarly bright to contend with the extroverted exterior and achieve a relationship of equals. In the entry hall, maize wallpaper, apricot curtains, a Day-Glo orange pillow, and a frog-green vase keep the intensity at a fever pitch. In the pale foam-green living room, color migrates off the walls and concentrates in the sofas and chairs, whose vivid upholstery has the collective effect of a room-wide bouquet. The vivid palette brings the outdoors in.

Because we're used to seeing bright colors in regions with bright natural light, bold combinations and high contrasts imply greater illumination. Strong colors have become lamps themselves, making a room feel warmer. Even in cool places outside the tropics, hot colors bring hot spots to mind.

PAGE 227: On the facade of this sun-soaked house, colors are saturated enough to compete with the sky. The purple on the door is no shrinking violet, and yellow is its perfect complement. The cacophony of color and pattern in this living room, LEFT, actually resolves into two complementary colors—orange and green—that extend even to the painting hung over the sofa.

A painting of a luminous subject, such as a pool, LEFT, can seem to create a light source where there is none. OPPOSITE: In a palette that ranges from dusty rose to delphinium blue, patterns of equal weight balance the decorating equation.

BELOW: Rather than recede into the landscape, this house is as vivid as a tropical fruit. French doors open the interior to the pool, the garden, and the light.

A still life of objects arranged on a mahogany chest, ABOVE, balances color and pattern. OPPOSITE: Complementary colors like orange and green heighten each other and establish the poles of a vibrant palette.

Rural Wisconsin

You would expect Alfred Lunt and Lynn Fontanne, the greatest acting team in American theatrical history, to know something about how to create an effect. Every summer, after the curtain fell on their latest production, they would head back to Genesee Depot, Wisconsin, and their beloved home, Ten Chimneys, where friends like Noel Coward, Helen Hayes, and Laurence Olivier would come to stay for weeks at a time. The white stucco and clapboard house—large and rambling, with shuttered casement windows—still looks fundamentally modest, yet first-time guests never failed to gasp when they stepped through the front door. ❡ Inside is a fantasy that rivals any stage set. Swedish furnishings (in a nod to Lunt's ancestry) conjure up sunlit midsummer nights, with segues to Renaissance Italy, Colonial America, and eighteenth-century France thrown in through other antiques. Some of the pieces are

PAGE 235: The transplanted Swedish vernacular found its purest expression in the Cottage, a converted chicken coop, where Alfred Lunt did much of the decorative painting himself. Architectural details such as a dado and chair rail are mimicked in paint. If a pattern is regular and repetitive, the eye registers it as a field of color.

Every surface turns to pattern in the main room of the Cottage where the furnishings seem to step out of a Swedish folktale. The nonfocused, all-over narrative pattern confounds space.

236: Color and Light

The white folly near the pool holds dressing rooms. Every year, Lunt planted red geraniums. Red defines an edge better than any other color, and brimming pots border the stone path.

actually props plucked from their plays. But that's not all that makes the house remarkable. Completely unique is the way almost every surface in each room has been touched and transformed—either embellished with hand-painted figures, garnished with gilt, adorned with mirrors, or simply polished with coat after coat of satiny paint. Cut crystal chandeliers and gleaming Chinese porcelain augment the reflections and magnify every bit of light.

Set designer Claggett Wilson, who arrived one summer and stayed more than a year, did all the decorative painting—with some help from Lunt, who was responsible for the Adam and Eve mural (with Fontanne modeling for both figures). Lunt also painted many of the folk-art motifs in the rustic Cottage, which housed his mother until she died. Sometimes the designs creep up onto the ceiling, which creates a vertiginous 360-degree surround. The swirl of all-over color and pattern evokes the gradations visible right outside in the midst of nature. The eye dances among the patterns, and the full spectrum of color brings out the warmth in the clear rural light, creating the illusion of light even when it's not there. The same process occurs when we look at an Impressionist painting and resolve fragments of color into a "lit" surface. The Lunts instinctively created a scintillating atmosphere. Their tangible legacy, Ten Chimneys, is a confection of color, light, and air.

At the top of the entrance hall, ABOVE, motifs cut from wallpaper and glued to the walls match the coral carpeting. TOP: The original white-painted farmhouse grew as rooms were added over time.

Light softened by sheer curtains, ABOVE, plays across the surface of the drawing room murals, painted by Claggett Wilson, which cover the walls and climb up the ceiling. OPPOSITE: On close approach, the scintillating blur of color resolves into separate shades of salmon, yellow, gray, green, and cream.

Because the colors are close in value, each panel—including this glimpse of Moses amid the bullrushes, ABOVE, reads as a whole.

Illusion and reality interweave in the dining room. It is hard to tell where the painted ceiling stops and the walls begin, LEFT. White Gustavian chairs and cut crystal send back the light. ABOVE: Fluttering candle flames multiply in the rococo swirls of a gilded mirror.

On Lynn Fontanne's dressing table, glass flowers twine amid the lights and cut the glare of the bare bulbs. OPPOSITE: In the Helen Hayes bedroom, the mural's gray shades move closer to cool blue when seen beside the warm yellow chest.

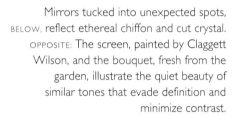

Mirrors tucked into unexpected spots, BELOW, reflect ethereal chiffon and cut crystal. OPPOSITE: The screen, painted by Claggett Wilson, and the bouquet, fresh from the garden, illustrate the quiet beauty of similar tones that evade definition and minimize contrast.

A subtle array of shades revolving around cloudy whites creates a vaporous atmosphere in a guest bedroom, ABOVE. Diaphanous curtains filter the sun, and the fretwork over the windows catches any stray gleam of light. Soft sheepskins stitched together cover the floor.

A Patina Notebook

Patinas are acquired, not bought; they happen gradually over years in a silent compact between man-made structures and the processes of nature. The sun's rays take a toll on surfaces—metal dulls; paint cracks and finally flakes. Distressed walls and materials possess a dimension that eludes the newest products straight off the assembly line. The physical evidence of time, light, and weather is visually pleasing because variegation replicates effects found in nature. What intrigues the eye is that something has gone slightly wild and veered out of our control, implying a larger order and disorder. We are attracted to objects that embody a sense of age because with it comes character. It's reassuring to see that our work has survived, transformed into something even more rich and strange.

Abrasion

From the point of view of a green wooden fence in the high desert, nature is sandpaper. Cycles of sun, rain, wind, and airborne dirt off the dry lake bed nearby abrade the painted surface to reveal multiple truths—the marks of a circular saw, knots in the grain, threads of vestigial paint in the cracks. Aluminum trailers corrode. Even the aquamarine shell of an abandoned swimming pool, meant to be impervious to water, succumbs. Nature reclaims what man has made and exposes once again its elemental character.

Adhesion

The weathering process does not merely take away, it can also add to—as demonstrated by the exterior surfaces of these barns, which have acquired a botanical overlay. At any point in time, millions of plant spores are in the air, looking for lodging. Sunlight and moisture conspire with the spores to loosen whitewash and soften barn siding in preparation for their landing. If the atmospheric conditions are right, lichen and moss take hold, veiling entire walls and shrouding sharp corners. Man's laborious constructions gradually revert to nature.

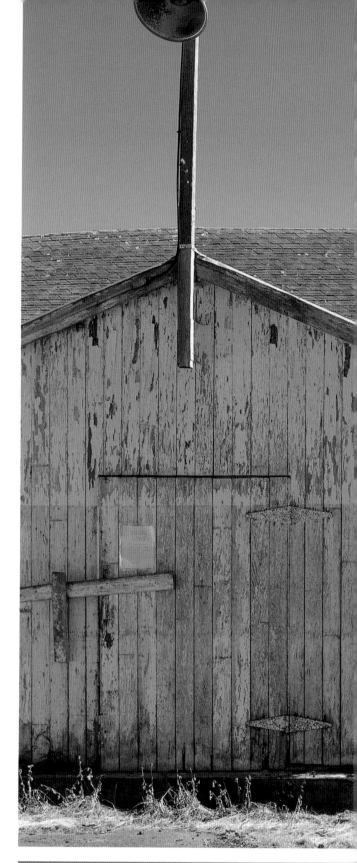

Application

The pentimento of myriad layers of paint on a wall creates visual texture and depth within a single plane. Fugitive pigments on surfaces permeable to water set off organic processes with a life of their own. Over the years, multiple applications of complementary colors wear at uneven rates. One layer delaminates in certain spots to reveal another. Faux finishers employ their art to capture and even accelerate the progress of time. In re-creating these effects, authenticity depends on the illusion of randomness and complexity, so prevalent outdoors. Patina brings man and his artifacts closer to nature.

Index